P9-DUD-820

COUNTDOWN TO SPACE

GALILEO SPACECRAFT
Mission to Jupiter

Michael D. Cole

Series Advisor:
John E. McLeaish
Chief, Public Information Office, retired,
NASA Johnson Space Center

Enslow Publishers, Inc.

44 Fadem Road	PO Box 38
Box 699	Aldershot
Springfield, NJ 07081	Hants GU12 6BP
USA	UK

http://www.enslow.com

Copyright © 1999 by Enslow Publishers, Inc.

All rights reserved.

No part of this book may be reproduced by any means without the written permission of the publisher.

Library of Congress Cataloging-in-Publication Data

Cole, Michael D.
    Galileo spacecraft : mission to Jupiter / Michael D. Cole.
      p.   cm. — (Countdown to space)
    Includes bibliographical references and index.
    Summary: Discusses the travel of the Galileo spacecraft from its launch to its orbit around Jupiter, explaining the goals and accomplishments of the mission.
    ISBN 0-7660-1119-4
    1. Jupiter (Planet)—Exploration—Juvenile literature. 2. Galileo Project—Juvenile literature. 3. Jupiter probes—Juvenile literature. [1. Galileo Project. 2. Jupiter (Planet)—Exploration.] I. Title. II. Series.
    QB661.C68   1999
    629.43'545—dc21   98-3627
                                        CIP
                                        AC

Printed in the United States of America

10 9 8 7 6 5 4 3 2 1

To Our Readers: All Internet addresses in this book were active and appropriate when we went to press. Any comments or suggestions can be sent by e-mail to Comments@enslow.com or to the address on the back cover.
The Publisher

Illustration Credits: National Aeronautics and Space Administration (NASA), STScI, p. 30; NASA/JPL, pp. 4, 7, 9, 11, 14, 16, 18, 19, 21, 24, 25, 27, 29, 34, 36, 39; STScI, J. Spencer (Lowell Observatory), and NASA, p. 37.

Cover Illustration: NASA/JPL (foreground); Raghvendra Sahai and John Trauger (JPL), the WFPC2 science team, NASA, and AURA/STScI (background).

Cover Photo: The Galileo probe parachutes through the thick clouds of Jupiter's atmosphere.

629.43
COL
1999

CONTENTS

The Galileo *spacecraft undergoes testing before its launch.*

1
Messages from Jupiter

The unmanned spacecraft *Galileo* traveled at nearly one hundred thousand miles per hour through the lonely darkness of space. It had already traveled more than two billion miles. Its path had taken it on a winding course through the part of the solar system where the planets Mercury, Venus, Earth, and Mars orbited around the sun. Now it was nearing the final destination of its journey.

The date was December 7, 1995. *Galileo* was about to become the first spacecraft to enter orbit around our solar system's largest planet, Jupiter. Its mission was to conduct a two-year study of the planet and its moons.

As it traveled through space, millions of miles from any human being, *Galileo* had the full attention of thousands of scientists and engineers on Earth.

"Today is the big day and everyone has been asking me how I feel," said Rosaly Lopes-Gautier, a scientist on the *Galileo* mission. "It has been a very long journey for *Galileo*, but also for myself."[1]

Lopes-Gautier remembered her childhood in Brazil. Even as a little girl she had wanted to work for the National Aeronautics and Space Administration (NASA) and take part in the exploration of space. She went to college in England and earned a degree in astronomy. Later she earned a Ph.D. in planetary geology and became interested in the study of volcanoes.

"Volcanoes are just great," Lopes-Gautier said, "and seeing an eruption live is one of the most exciting things that anyone can do."[2]

At about the time she began her study of volcanoes, NASA's *Voyager* spacecraft flew by Jupiter. On one of Jupiter's moons, Io (pronounced *Eye-oh*), *Voyager* discovered the presence of active volcanoes.

Lopes-Gautier began to work for NASA's Jet Propulsion Laboratory (JPL) in Pasadena, California, and was assigned to the *Galileo* mission in 1991. Because of her background in the study of volcanoes, her job was to plan the scientific observations the spacecraft would make during its flyby of Io where the volcanic activity had been observed. It was a tremendous amount of work. But Lopes-Gautier was doing what she had dreamed of doing since she was a little girl.

"You really have to be philosophical when you work

on a space mission," she said. "You know that everything is at the forefront of technology and something can go wrong. You have to risk working for a long time on something that may come to nothing. But I have no regrets, and I will be very happy when we get into orbit tonight."[3]

The time was approaching when *Galileo*'s engines would fire to slow the spacecraft, putting it into orbit around Jupiter. But getting the spacecraft into orbit around Jupiter was not the only event for the *Galileo* team on this important day.

Galileo *was the first spacecraft to orbit Jupiter.*

Galileo was actually in two separate parts already: the atmospheric probe and the orbiter. The atmospheric probe would go down, or descend, through Jupiter's atmosphere. The orbiter would remain in orbit around the planet.

The atmospheric probe had separated from the orbiter 147 days earlier, as planned. The orbiter and probe had flown the rest of the way to Jupiter on separate courses. In a very short time the *Galileo* atmospheric probe would begin its descent into the thick upper atmosphere of Jupiter. During its descent, it would relay information about the planet to the orbiter.[4]

"In a way, I've been waiting for this day for more than seventeen years," said Steven Tyler, an engineer on the project. "I started working on *Galileo* in August of 1978."

The mission had taken ten years longer to get off the ground than Tyler and others had originally planned.

"I've spent several years working on *Galileo*," Tyler said. "If *Galileo* is a success, I'm going to feel that this work has paid off."[5]

The probe would use its cone-shaped heat shield to slow itself before parachuting through the planet's thick clouds. As planned, the probe would eventually be crushed by the heavy pressure of Jupiter's atmosphere. The signal would be lost, and the probe's mission would be over.

"The problems of probe entry and survival . . . and

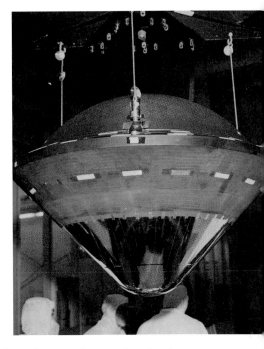

The assembled Galileo *probe is ready for its mission.*

of the relay link, are significant," Tyler said. He hoped that the probe would relay some good information to the orbiter about what types of clouds existed in Jupiter's atmosphere before the signal was lost. "I wonder what *Galileo* will discover. I suspect that the probe will find something surprising."

As the time drew nearer for the probe to begin its descent, Tyler was nervous and full of questions.

"Will we hear anything useful from the probe?" he wondered. "Will the heat shield work? Will the parachute work? Will the radio link work?"[6]

Excitement and anticipation spread throughout JPL. News reporters were crowding into the auditorium to await news of the important signals from the spacecraft. Radio signals travel at the speed of light, which is about 186,000 miles per second. At that speed, it would take fifty-two minutes for *Galileo*'s radio signal to travel the distance between Jupiter and Earth. The scientists, engineers, and managers waited in the control rooms.

Four hundred million miles away, the probe was

descending through Jupiter's atmosphere, relaying its scientific data to the *Galileo* orbiter above. While the orbiter recorded the probe's data, it sent the signal back to Earth confirming the probe's successful descent.[7]

Fifty-two minutes later the signal was received at JPL. Leslie Tamppari, another scientist with the *Galileo* project, had volunteered to answer reporters' questions.

"I was so nervous while waiting for confirmation that the probe that we dropped into Jupiter's atmosphere was working fine," Tamppari said. "The signal came about six minutes later than I had been expecting, so I was getting very fearful that something had gone wrong. When the confirmation finally came through, I was nearly in tears from the joy of knowing that we had done it!"

Tamppari was not the only one excited by the news.

"When the signal came through, everyone cheered and hugged each other!" she added. "The press started snapping pictures of all of us cheering and later came up to interview some of us!"[8]

About an hour later the probe was lost, as planned, in the dense atmosphere of Jupiter. Its signal to the orbiter had stopped. But it had accomplished its mission. The scientific data from its descent was safely stored on tape aboard the orbiter. The data would be relayed to Earth later. But first the all-important engine burn to put *Galileo* into orbit around Jupiter was coming up.

Galileo's direction toward the planet had already been

changed by flying past Io. As mission scientists had planned, Io's gravity had altered the orbiter's course, helping to set it up for orbit around the planet. The orbiter turned to prepare for a forty-nine-minute burn of its main rocket, which would insert *Galileo* into orbit around Jupiter.

After a six-year journey, covering more than two billion miles, the time clicked down to the precise second when the engines needed to begin the burn. At that exact moment, the main rocket engines on *Galileo* ignited.

Again, the people at JPL waited anxiously for the important signal to arrive.

The exciting mission began when Galileo *was launched from Cape Canaveral, Florida, aboard the space shuttle* Atlantis.

Leslie Tamppari was still in the auditorium with the reporters.

"We got the signal that the big engines aboard Galileo started firing right on time," she said. "That was a relief too, since if they didn't work right we would have become a flyby mission instead of an orbiting mission." Everything went perfectly. "Forty-nine minutes later," Tamppari said, "the engines stopped, right on time."[9]

The *Galileo* spacecraft and the thousands of people who had worked on it had accomplished their primary goal. The journey had begun when *Galileo* was launched from Cape Canaveral aboard the space shuttle *Atlantis* on October 18, 1989. Now, *Galileo* was finally in orbit around Jupiter.

"We've started to get some data back from the probe," Tamppari said days later. "I can't wait to find out what interesting things they have found! It's so great to finally be in orbit around Jupiter!"[10]

2

The Sunlike Planet

The planet Jupiter is by far the largest planet in the solar system. While Earth is nearly eight thousand miles wide from one side to the other, Jupiter is more than eighty-eight thousand miles across. The planet is so large that more than one thousand Earths could fit inside it. In addition, all of the other eight planets in the solar system, including Saturn and its rings, could be placed together inside Jupiter.[1]

But why send a spacecraft to Jupiter? What can Jupiter tell scientists that could be of any importance to people on Earth? Jupiter may be able to help answer many of our questions about the universe.

Like the sun's, Jupiter's main chemical components

are hydrogen and helium. The sun has nine orbiting planets. Jupiter has sixteen orbiting moons.

"In many ways, Jupiter is like a miniature solar system in itself," said Dr. Wesley T. Huntress, NASA's associate administrator for space science. Because of the similarities between Jupiter and the sun, Dr. Huntress added that the *Galileo* mission "should uncover new clues about how the sun and the planets formed, and about how they continue to interact and evolve."[2]

Jupiter is producing one and a half times more heat

Jupiter is so large that more than one thousand Earths could fit inside it.

than it absorbs from the sun. This means that deep within the planet's layers of clouds and gases, it is producing its own energy. Scientists believe that it could be producing this energy in the same way that the sun produces its energy. If this is so, the planet Jupiter could be in the early phases of becoming a star.[3]

Unlike the clouds on Earth, which are made of floating droplets of water or ice, Jupiter's clouds consist of frozen bits of gases. The most common gases in Jupiter's clouds are ammonia and methane. These clouds completely circle the planet in bands that scientists believe are thousands of miles deep. Storms and high winds rage continually in these clouds. The temperature inside these clouds is extremely cold, at about −150°C (−240°F).

One of the most fascinating features about Jupiter is its Great Red Spot. For more than three hundred years, this rotating hurricane-like storm has been observed circling through the planet's atmosphere. The reason this storm has lasted for so long is not known. Three planets the size of Earth could fit inside the Great Red Spot.[4]

Jupiter's core lies beneath as much as twenty thousand miles of clouds and liquid hydrogen. It is not known if this core is solid, like the rock and soil of Earth's crust, or partly molten, like the magma in Earth's mantle. Either way, it would be extremely hot. It would also be under a tremendous amount of pressure from the

This Great Red Spot image contains possible thunderstorm clouds, shown in the white square.

deep layers of gases and liquid hydrogen surrounding the planet.

A spacecraft could never land on Jupiter because there is nothing to land *on*. It would simply be engulfed and crushed by the planet's thick layer of liquid hydrogen. Life as we know it could never exist on such a planet.

Another subject of great curiosity and importance to scientists is the sixteen moons that orbit the giant planet. The four largest moons of Jupiter were discovered by the Italian astronomer Galileo Galilei in

1610. He is the astronomer for whom the *Galileo* spacecraft is named. Because of his discovery of the moons Io, Europa, Ganymede, and Callisto, these moons are called the Galilean moons.

The Galilean moons are so large that if they were orbiting the sun we would think of them as planets. Each one of them is much larger than the planet Pluto. Because of their size, they are easily seen from Earth with a telescope.

The brightest of these moons, Europa, is covered with white ice that appears to be cracked and grooved over its entire surface. Scientists want to know whether this ice is composed of frozen water or some other combination of frozen elements. If it is water, the water could possibly contain life.

Ganymede, the largest of Jupiter's moons, has craters and deep grooves. It appears to be so old that the crust has cracked and moved sideways, creating many surface ridges. Callisto is the darkest of the Galilean moons. Its brown surface is dappled everywhere with bright white spots where meteorites have splashed fresh ice from the moon's interior out onto the surface.[5]

Io is the same size as the moon that orbits Earth, but it looks nothing like Earth's moon. Volcanoes are present on Io, and they have coated the surface with sulfur compounds. These compounds cover the moon in patches of color ranging from red to yellow. Some astronomers call Io the pizza moon, because its

Four of Jupiter's moons—Io, Europa, Ganymede, and Callisto—are large enough to be seen from Earth with a telescope.

unusually colored surface gives the appearance of cheese and tomato sauce, with the volcanoes hinting at pepperonis.[6]

On March 2, 1972, NASA launched *Pioneer 10* to Jupiter. It passed within eighty-one thousand miles of the planet in December 1973. *Pioneer 11* followed in April 1973, making its flyby almost twenty-seven thousand miles from Jupiter in December 1974.

Pioneer 10 and *11* were not sophisticated spacecraft. Before sending more complex instruments to the planet, scientists and engineers first wanted to know whether a spacecraft could survive the journey through the rocky asteroid belt that exists between Mars and Jupiter. NASA also sent *Pioneer 10* and *11* through Jupiter's powerful magnetic field to test whether the spacecraft could withstand the planet's intense radiation.

Both Pioneers survived their journey through the asteroid belt. They arrived to take many pictures of the

This color-enhanced photo shows Europa's icy plains in blue.

ALBUQUERQUE ACADEMY
LIBRARY

clouds and of the Great Red Spot of Jupiter. The spacecraft also continued to function in the presence of Jupiter's high radiation. The radiation levels were measured to be a thousand times the lethal dose for an astronaut.[7]

Voyager 1 and *Voyager 2* were launched in late summer of 1977. The Voyagers took so many pictures of Jupiter that scientists were able to piece them together and make movies. These movies showed the movements of clouds and weather systems on the planet. At this time, volcanoes were discovered on the large moon Io. On the dark side of Jupiter, the Voyagers took pictures of lightning flashes ten thousand times more powerful than any that occur on Earth.

The two spacecraft discovered something previously unknown about the planet: a faint ring around it. The ring is composed of tiny bits of rock and dust. It is nothing like the complex system of colorful rings surrounding Saturn. In fact, it is so dim that humans without telescopes would not see the ring even from a spaceship in orbit around Jupiter. But it is there.[8]

To learn more about the planet, scientists needed more sophisticated spacecraft. Weeks after the second Voyager spacecraft was launched to Jupiter in September 1977, Congress gave its approval to the *Galileo* project. The approval was only the beginning of a very long journey back to Jupiter. It was a longer journey than anyone imagined.

Io is the most volcanic body in the solar system. It is sometimes referred to as the pizza moon because of its appearance.

"I joined the *Galileo* project as an engineer . . . in 1980," said Dave Atkinson, a member of the science team for the *Galileo* probe. As the spacecraft neared its destination in September 1995, Atkinson looked back on the project. "During the last fifteen years I've seen *Galileo* canceled by Congress and then reinstated."

He also waited through many delays in the

development of the space shuttle that carried *Galileo* into space. Each delay caused a redesign of the *Galileo* mission.

"I watched as the launch date was moved from 1984 . . . to 1986 . . . to 1989," Atkinson said. "In 1986 *Galileo* was at the Cape and preparing for a spring launch when the *Challenger* accident occurred." The explosion of the space shuttle *Challenger*, which killed all seven astronauts aboard, caused a lengthy delay for *Galileo* as well as delays for other space missions.[9]

After the long process of designing and constructing the spacecraft and the years of problems and delays, *Galileo* finally sat on the launchpad at Cape Canaveral. It was time to launch *Galileo* into space to begin its journey to Jupiter.

3

Voyage to Jupiter

On the pad at Cape Canaveral, *Galileo* was housed within the payload bay of the space shuttle *Atlantis*. *Atlantis* would carry *Galileo* into orbit.

Atlantis roared off the pad on October 18, 1989, finally carrying the sophisticated spacecraft into space. Release from the shuttle's payload bay went perfectly. When *Galileo* had cleared the area of the shuttle, the command was given to fire its rocket booster. Minutes later the rocket booster successfully pushed *Galileo* out of Earth orbit. The spacecraft was on its way to Jupiter.

After its first four months in space, *Galileo* had traveled inward toward the sun to arrive at the planet Venus on February 10, 1990. Using *Galileo's* instruments, scientists believe they confirmed the presence of

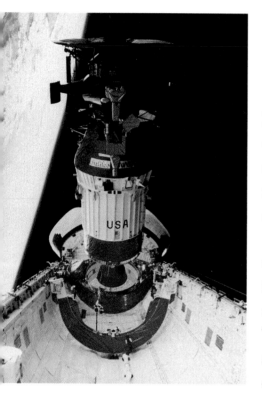

Galileo is released from the space shuttle's payload bay to begin its journey to Jupiter.

lightning in the atmosphere of Venus. Cameras aboard the spacecraft also secured the first images of midlevel clouds on Venus.

On December 8, 1990, *Galileo* made its first Earth flyby, coming within 620 miles of Earth's atmosphere. The spacecraft's journey was already more than one year old, yet it would still be five more years before *Galileo* would arrive at Jupiter. As a result of the first Earth flyby, *Galileo* picked up speed and headed out beyond the orbital path of Mars and into a region of the asteroid belt.

All seemed to be going well with *Galileo* when the mission engineers got their first surprise. On April 11, 1991, the spacecraft's high-gain antenna, mounted on top of *Galileo*, was designed to unfurl like an umbrella. In this open position it would form a dish that would transmit data back to Earth during the spacecraft's encounter with Jupiter. Until this day, controllers at JPL had used the spacecraft's much slower low-gain antenna.

The more delicate high-gain antenna had been kept closed beneath a sun shade to protect it from the sun's rays, because the sun's rays are much more intense near Venus and in the inner solar system.[1]

Unfortunately, the antenna failed to open.

"I couldn't believe it when the antenna didn't open," said Neil Ausman, *Galileo's* mission director. "I did not anticipate that failure mode. But I thought, 'We'll fix it anyway.'"[2]

Over the next several weeks, a team of more than one

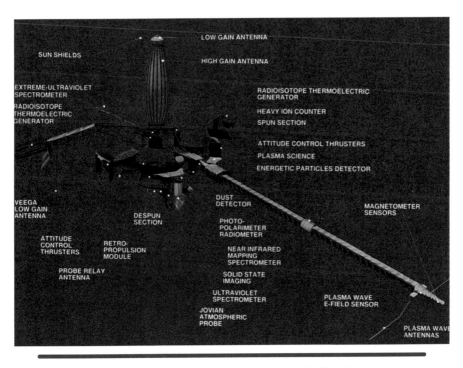

Astronomers did not anticipate problems with Galileo's instruments. However, on April 11, 1991, Galileo's high-gain antenna would not open into position.

hundred technical experts attempted to solve the problem of getting the antenna to open. The experts concluded that the most likely cause of the problem was that a number of the antenna ribs themselves were stuck. The antenna ribs are like the folding metal rods that hold an umbrella open. All attempts to open the antenna failed.

Without the high-gain antenna, the spacecraft would be unable to transmit data to mission scientists as quickly as they had planned. Also, with only the low-gain antenna working, *Galileo's* signal would not be received as clearly by the Deep Space Network of receivers on Earth. Failure of the high-gain antenna could affect some parts of the mission. Scientists and engineers would have to make the mission work with the low-gain antenna only. Mission director Ausman refused to be discouraged by the setback.

"When I finally concluded we weren't going to [open the high-gain antenna], I saw that we could still have a good mission with the low-gain antenna," he said. "Through it all, I never had time to sulk. We had too much work to do."[3]

Six months after the mission team had faced the antenna problem, *Galileo* entered the asteroid belt. On October 29, 1991, *Galileo* became the first spacecraft ever to encounter an asteroid, a large rocklike object orbiting around the sun. The asteroid belt exists in an area between the orbital paths of Mars and Jupiter. *Galileo* passed within one thousand miles of the rocky asteroid Gaspra, which was about twelve miles long and about seven and a half miles wide.

Pictures showed that Gaspra has many craters and a thin covering of dirt and dust. The spacecraft also detected the possible presence of a magnetic field around the asteroid.[4]

Flying on its curved path through the asteroid belt, *Galileo* began to circle back into the inner solar system toward a second encounter with Earth. In December

These Deep Space Network antennas, located in Australia, receive data from Galileo.

1992, *Galileo* passed between Earth and the Moon. Mission scientists made some important studies of the Moon. *Galileo* was able to do a complete mapping of the Moon's north pole region, called the Imbrium impact basin.

Galileo also made a collection of color-enhanced photographs that highlighted different chemical properties of the Moon's surface. These pictures told scientists things about the Moon they had never known before. The images showed them that volcanic activity had taken place on the Moon much earlier than scientists had believed. Also, a meteor or asteroid impact on the Moon long ago had thrown out huge amounts of rock and debris that eventually settled over the Moon's entire surface.

Completing this second swing around Earth, *Galileo* gained more speed. The spacecraft was then set on the long path that would carry it completely through the asteroid belt and out to the giant planet Jupiter.

Galileo once again entered the asteroid belt. There was some chance that it would actually collide with one of the many smaller uncharted asteroids within the asteroid belt. Fortunately, this did not occur. Instead, on August 28, 1993, *Galileo's* instruments recorded a second asteroid encounter. *Galileo* flew by the asteroid Ida, which was about thirty-four miles wide and had a very irregular shape.

More important, *Galileo* discovered a smaller object

in orbit around Ida. Ida had its own moon! This moon, later named Dactyl, was the first moon ever to be discovered in orbit around an asteroid.

Earlier in 1993, astronomers Eugene and Carolyn Shoemaker and David Levy had discovered a comet they later named Comet Shoemaker-Levy 9 (it was the ninth comet they had discovered). The comet was in fragments, and as scientists calculated the orbit of these fragments, it was predicted that in July of 1994 a number of them would slam into the atmosphere of Jupiter.[5] After the many problems and delays in getting *Galileo* into space, an incredible stroke of luck had placed the spacecraft in a position at just the right time to observe the comet's impact.

"*Galileo's* mission has been interesting already," said

Galileo discovered that the asteroid Ida had its own moon, shown as the small white image at the right.

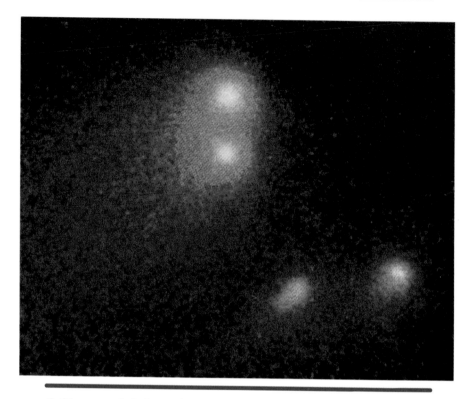

Galileo *recorded data of the Comet Shoemaker-Levy 9's collision with Jupiter. The Hubble Space Telescope took this picture of the comet.*

mission engineer Steven Tyler. "The earlier mission would have been at the wrong time to make even a limited observation of Shoemaker-Levy. We [also] might not have discovered a moon about an asteroid."[6]

The impact of the Shoemaker-Levy comet into Jupiter's atmosphere in July 1994 was the biggest fireworks show in the solar system. Still 121 million miles away, *Galileo* pointed its instruments at Jupiter to record the impacts. The explosion of one of the comet fragments caused a fireball 1,600 miles high and 5,000 miles wide. The fireball from the explosion was larger than the entire Earth.

Galileo took pictures and recorded other data of the event. The Hubble Space Telescope, in orbit around Earth, also took pictures of the comet impacts in Jupiter's atmosphere. Other telescopes on Earth were turned toward Jupiter and did their best to record the impacts. It was an exciting event for astronomers.

"Nature has hit us a home run," said astronomer Levy. Data recorded from the comet's collision with Jupiter could help scientists answer questions about how the solar system was formed. It could also tell them what might happen if a comet ever struck Earth.[7]

In July 1995, *Galileo*'s atmospheric probe separated as planned from the orbiter. Once separated, the two spacecraft flew on different courses the rest of the way to the planet.

Just weeks before the probe and the orbiter were scheduled to finally arrive at Jupiter, another problem arose. Once again something had happened on *Galileo* that threatened the success of the mission.

4

Galileo at Jupiter

On October 11, 1995, less than two months before *Galileo*'s scheduled arrival at Jupiter, the spacecraft's tape recorder malfunctioned. The tape recorder was an important mechanism to the mission. It stored data from the spacecraft's instruments and then transmitted that data to Earth. After recording an image of Jupiter, signals from the spacecraft showed that the tape recorder had failed to stop rewinding. The recorder had rewound to the beginning of the tape, but it would not click out of rewind mode. The recorder was stuck in this position for fifteen hours, possibly weakening the end of the tape.

Engineers at JPL finally got the recorder working again, but there was fear that the end of the tape had been damaged and that further use might tear it. To protect the section of tape that might have been damaged, engineers commanded the recorder to wind an extra twenty-five times. The tape was never again to be rewound to the beginning of the reel, and that part of the tape was off-limits for all further recording.[1]

The tape recorder problem affected some plans for *Galileo's* arrival at Jupiter. There was now a reduced amount of room on the tape in addition to the slow data-transmission speed of the low-gain antenna. Therefore, mission planners canceled all of *Galileo's* scheduled observations as it made its closest flyby of Jupiter's moon Io. That day, the recorder was instead completely devoted to recording data relayed to it from the probe as it descended through Jupiter's atmosphere.

December 7, 1995, was the big day. The probe's descent through Jupiter's upper atmosphere began right on schedule. It transmitted important scientific data about the planet's atmosphere to the orbiter, and the orbiter's tape recorder stored the data perfectly. About an hour later, when the probe's transmission signal ceased, the data was safely on the tape aboard the orbiter.

The orbiter then turned and prepared for the engine burn that would finally place it into orbit around Jupiter. Forty-nine minutes later, the signal came through that the engine burn was completed. The news that the *Galileo* team had all been waiting for was confirmed. After six years and 2.3 billion miles of space travel through the solar system, *Galileo* was in orbit around the planet Jupiter!

It was a personal victory for everyone involved with the mission.

"It has taken a while for it to sink in that the spacecraft is actually in orbit at Jupiter," said Lou D'Amario, an engineer on *Galileo*'s navigation team. "I feel relief and a tremendous sense of satisfaction that [it has] been completed successfully. To think that I was fortunate enough to be able to participate in getting *Galileo* to Jupiter is like a dream come true."[2]

Galileo's probe parachutes through Jupiter's thick clouds.

Robert Gounley, a member of the orbiter engineering team, related this story:

> In one corner of JPL's main plaza, a large black sign shows a map of the solar system. On it are movable symbols for the planets and the spacecraft JPL flies. Since *Galileo*'s launch . . . everyone . . . watched *Galileo*'s symbol loop around the diagram, leaving a dashed-line trail behind it. . . . For the past three years, the trail led directly to Jupiter. Each day, Galileo's symbol and Jupiter's symbol inched closer and closer. . . . This morning, a glorious Californian autumn day, someone tacked a small sign onto the map. It said, "BINGO!"[3]

For mission scientist Claudia Alexander, the success of the atmospheric probe and *Galileo*'s insertion into orbit were satisfying for other reasons.

"The best part was that my mother finally connected with what I have been devoted to for the past few years," Alexander said. Her mother had seen stories about the spacecraft's arrival on the nightly news. "She said, 'Ohhhh. Is that what you do. . . . We're going to learn all these exciting things about Jupiter for the first time. . . . This is really exciting.'"[4]

"The probe detected extremely strong winds and very intense turbulence during its descent through Jupiter's thick atmosphere," said probe project scientist Richard Young. "The probe also discovered an intense new radiation belt approximately thirty-one thousand

The efforts of many people, including these technicians who assembled the probe, made the Galileo *mission a success.*

miles above Jupiter's cloud tops, and [an almost complete] absence of lightning."[5]

NASA associate administrator for space science, Dr. Wesley Huntress, was impressed with the data relayed to Earth by the *Galileo* probe and orbiter.

"The quality of the *Galileo* probe data exceeds all of our most optimistic predictions," he said. "It will allow the scientific community to develop valuable new insights into the formation and evolution of our solar system, and the origins of life within it."[6]

Galileo has made some stunning discoveries during its orbits of the Jupiter system. Many of these discoveries concerned the unusual properties of Jupiter's larger moons. The presence of large metallic cores were detected from instrument readings of the moons Io, Europa, and Ganymede. Io was also shown to have been turned white in some areas by sulfur dioxide blown from active volcanoes on the moon's surface. These volcanoes had changed the moon's appearance dramatically since the Voyager spacecraft had taken pictures of it only seventeen years earlier. Changes occurred even during the time of the *Galileo* mission itself.

Active volcanoes on Io's surface (as seen on the left of Io) have been studied by Galileo.

Ganymede, which is almost the size of Mars, was discovered to possess its own magnetic field. It is the first known moon in the solar system to possess a magnetic field. *Galileo* also discovered an atmosphere of hydrogen and carbon dioxide around the moon Callisto. The orbiter took pictures of what appeared to be water ice floes on the icy surface of the moon Europa. The movement hinted at the possibility of liquid water below Europa's surface, a condition that scientists believe might make the development of life possible.

Galileo's images of Jupiter's Great Red Spot showed the circular storm moving counterclockwise at a speed of 250 miles per hour. The storm was over sixteen thousand miles wide, a distance wider than two entire Earths. Images from *Galileo* are allowing scientists to measure the altitude of Jupiter's clouds and to study new details in the structure of the giant storm.[7]

Galileo was designed for a two-year mission of eleven orbits around the planet Jupiter. That mission was extended for two more years, continuing through the end of 1999.

This two-year extension includes three main phases. The first is a series of eight close flybys of the moon Europa. During these flybys, *Galileo* will make a study of the ice floes on Europa's surface. It will look for more evidence of an ocean under the icy surface. This series will take more than a year. The second phase includes a series of orbital maneuvers designed to put *Galileo* in an orbit close enough to Jupiter to fly near the moon Io. During these maneuvers, which will take six months, *Galileo* will make observations of the wind and storm patterns in Jupiter's top atmosphere layers. The third and final phase of the extended mission has *Galileo* making two flybys (as close as 350 miles) to the moon Io. The spacecraft will use the pair of flybys to make closer observations of the volcanic activity on the moon's surface.[8]

At the end of 1999, this extended mission will be completed. By that time, it is likely that the intense radiation around Jupiter will begin to cause electronic equipment aboard *Galileo* to fail. *Galileo*'s mission will officially end when mission controllers at JPL lose contact with the well-traveled space-craft.

Even after its mission controllers lose contact with

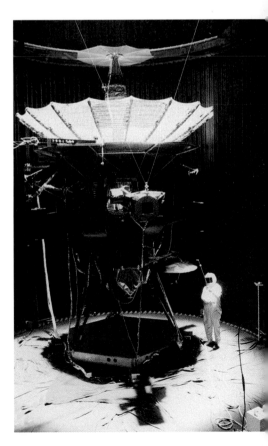

Before Galileo's *launch, scientists made sure it was ready for its task. The extended mission of* Galileo *will enable scientists to discover even more about Jupiter's moons and atmosphere.*

Galileo, the spacecraft will continue to orbit around Jupiter or one of its moons for a very long time. Though scientists and engineers will no longer be in contact with *Galileo,* the mission's contributions to our understanding of the universe will continue for years after its electronic signal has ceased.

As its influence continues, *Galileo's* silent orbits through the Jupiter system are a fitting monument to the dedication and commitment its team members showed to the exploration of space.

CHAPTER NOTES

Chapter 1. Messages from Jupiter

1. NASA K–12 Educational Resource, "Rosaly Lopes-Gautier field journal entry," *Online From Jupiter*, December 7, 1995, p. 1, <http://quest.arc.nasa.gov/galileo/bios/fjournals/gautier-ofj1.html> (July 10, 1998).

2. Ibid.

3. Ibid., pp. 1–2.

4. *Galileo* Press Kit, National Aeronautics and Space Administration, issued December 1995, pp. 2–3.

5. NASA K–12 Educational Resource, "Steven Tyler field journal entry," *Online From Jupiter*, December 7, 1995, pp. 1–2, <http://quest.arc.nasa.gov/galileo/bios/fjournals/tyler-ofj3.html> (July 10, 1998).

6. Ibid., p. 1.

7. NASA Press Release 96-54, *Galileo Scientists Report Changing Findings About Jupiter*, March 18, 1996, p. 2.

8. NASA K–12 Educational Resource, "Leslie Tamppari field journal entry," *Online From Jupiter*, December 11, 1995, p. 1, <http://quest.arc.nasa.gov/galileo/bios/fjournals/tamppari-ofj2.html> (July 10, 1998).

9. Ibid.

10. Ibid.

Chapter 2. The Sunlike Planet

1. Thomas R. Watters, *Planets: The Story of Our Solar System—From Earth to the Farthest Planet and Beyond* (New York: Macmillan, 1995), p. 128.

2. *Galileo* Press Kit, National Aeronautics and Space Administration, issued December 1995, p. 1.

3. Reta Beebe, *Jupiter: The Giant Planet* (Washington, D.C.: Smithsonian Institution Press, 1994), pp. 2, 8–9.

4. Ibid., p. 135.

5. Nigel Henbest, *The Planets: Portraits of New Worlds* (New York: Penguin Press, 1992), pp. 111–121.

6. Melvin Berger, Discovering Jupiter: *The Amazing Collision in Space* (New York: Scholastic, Inc., 1995), p. 33.

7. Henbest, p. 107.

8. Ibid., pp. 108–119.

9. NASA K–12 Educational Resource, "Dave Atkinson field journal entry," *Online From Jupiter*, September 27, 1995, p. 1, <http://quest.arc.nasa.gov/galileo/bios/fjournals/atkinson-ofj1.html> (July 10, 1998).

Chapter 3. Voyage to Jupiter

1. *Galileo* Press Kit, National Aeronautics and Space Administration, issued December 1995, p. 24.

2. Paul Weissman and Marcia Segura, "Galileo Arrives at Jupiter," *Astronomy*, January 1996, p. 39.

3. Ibid.

4. *Galileo* Press Kit, p. 20.

5. Reta Beebe, *Jupiter: The Giant Planet* (Washington, D.C.: Smithsonian Institution Press, 1994), pp. 215–217.

6. NASA K–12 Educational Resource, "Steven Tyler field journal entry," *Online From Jupiter*, December 7, 1995, p. 1, <http://quest.arc.nasa.gov/galileo/bios/fjournals/tyler-ofj3.html> (July 10, 1998).

7. Melvin Berger, *Discovering Jupiter: The Amazing Collision in Space* (New York: Scholastic Inc., 1995), p. 52.

Chapter 4. Galileo at Jupiter

1. *Galileo* Press Kit, National Aeronautics and Space Administration, issued December 1995, pp. 27–28.

2. NASA K–12 Educational Resource, "Lou D'Amario field journal entry," *Online From Jupiter*, December 13, 1995, p. 1, <http://quest.arc.nasa.gov/galileo/bios/fjournals/damario-ofj11.html> (July 10, 1998).

3. NASA K–12 Educational Resource, "Robert Gounley field journal entry," *Online From Jupiter*, December 8, 1995, p. 1, <http://quest.arc.nasa.gov/galileo/bios/fjournals/gounley-ofj6.html> (July 10, 1998).

4. NASA K–12 Educational Resource, "Claudia Alexander field journal entry," *Online From Jupiter*, December 11, 1995, p. 2, <http://quest.arc.nasa.gov/galileo/bios/ fjournals/alexander-ofj3.html> (July 10, 1998).

5. NASA Press Release 96-10, *Galileo Probe Suggests Planetary Science Reappraisal*, January 22, 1996, pp. 1–2.

6. Ibid.

7. NASA Press Release 96-164, *Jupiter's Europa Harbors Possible "Warm Ice" or Liquid Water*, August 13, 1996, pp. 3–4.

8. *Galileo Internet Home Page*, n.d. <http://www.jpl.nasa.gov/galileo/gem/> (July 10, 1998).

GLOSSARY

asteroid—A rocky object or minor moon that orbits around the sun. Many asteroids are contained within the asteroid belt, which lies between the orbital paths of Mars and Jupiter.

atmospheric probe—A spacecraft that descends through the atmosphere of a planet to make studies of the atmosphere and the planet's clouds and weather.

comet—A ball of ice and dust that travels in an irregular orbit around the sun.

high-gain antenna—An antenna that communicates electronic data at very high speeds and in a focused beam.

inner solar system—The area of the solar system closest to the sun that includes Mercury, Venus, Earth, Mars, and their orbits.

low-gain antenna—An antenna that communicates electronic data at relatively slow speeds and in a wide beam that make its signals less clear than high-gain antenna signals.

magnetic field—The area of space surrounding a planet or other large body where its magnetic force can be felt.

orbiter—A spacecraft that goes into orbit around a planet or other object in space.

outer solar system—The area of the solar system farthest from the sun, which includes the asteroid belt and the planets Jupiter, Saturn, Uranus, Neptune, Pluto, and their orbital paths.

payload bay—The area of the space shuttle where cargo is stored.

probe—A robotic spacecraft designed to explore space by making scientific observations of planets or other objects.

radiation—Energy emitted in the form of waves or particles.

FURTHER READING

Books

Beebe, Reta. *Jupiter: The Giant Planet*. Washington, D.C.: Smithsonian Institution Press, 1994.

Berger, Melvin. *Discovering Jupiter: The Amazing Collision in Space*. New York: Scholastic, Inc., 1995.

Fradin, Dennis Brindell. *Jupiter*. Chicago: Children's Press, 1989.

Hightower, Paul. *Galileo: Astronomer and Physicist*. Springfield, NJ: Enslow Publishers, Inc., 1997.

Rogers, John H. *The Giant Planet Jupiter*. New York: Cambridge University Press, 1995.

Internet Addresses

NASA/JPL. "Project Galileo: Bringing Jupiter to Earth." *Galileo Home Page*. n.d. <http://galileo.ivv.nasa.gov/> (July 17, 1998).

National Space Science Data Center. "Galileo Project Information." *Planetary Sciences*. November 28, 1997. <http://nssdc.gsf.nasa.gov/planetary/galileo.html> (July 17, 1998).

Planetary Science Institute. "Galileo Asteroid Studies." *Planetary Science Institute*. n.d. <http://www.psi.edu/galileo.html> (July 17, 1998).

INDEX